My People Was Music

Kirk Judd

Sheila-Na-Gig Editions

Russell, KY • USA

My People Was Music © 2021 Kirk Judd

ISBN 979-8-9855242-8-4

Library of Congress Control Number: 2014937335

Second Edition
Printed in the United States of America

www.sheilanagigblog.com

CREDITS

Many of these poems appeared previously in the chapbooks *Field of Vision*, 1986, by Aegina Press, and *Tao-Billy*, 1996, by Trillium Press. Some of the poems appeared previously in *Hill and Valley, The Illustrated Appalachian Intelligencer, The West Virginia Hillbilly, Venue, Grab-a-Nickel, BOGG, Tantra Press, Volunteer's Ink, Now & Then, Coming Together, Field Notes, Down Home, Trout Lines, Kestrel, Down the River, The Sow's Ear, Songs of the Hills, The Dickensonian, Appalachian Heritage, Coal: A Poetry Anthology, Wild Sweet Notes – 50 Years of West Virginia Poetry,* and *The Hamilton Stone Review.*

Photographs by Dave Lambert
Cover Design: Keith Davis
Back Cover Photo by Candace Jordan
Pen and Ink Drawing by Boyd Carr
Proofreader Barbara Smith

TABLE OF CONTENTS

For West Virginia

Poet

I am trajectory and flight –
The archer, arrow, and the bow –
The swift parabola of light –
And I the rising and the flow,
The falling feather of the cock,
The point, propulsion and the flood
Of blackbirds twanging from the nock,
And I the target and the blood.

—Louise McNeill

The High Country
Remembers Her Heritage

My people was music.
Their lives were poems
told in the old language
of earth and season,
rain and sun,
field and sweat,
stream and blood.

My people was music.
They come to this country
in fiddle cases thrown on the tide.
They burst on the shore
and notes was their babies
and they spread over the land,
moving up the valleys and the hollows
with the piping of the wind,
moving up the rivers and the runs
with the rhythm of the spawn,
the pulse of blood on membrane
beating—coming home to live,
coming home to die,
coming home to live,
coming home.

My people was music.
They throwed down roots
and growed up families and stayed.
Stand with your heart in the earth
and your hand in the sky
and hear 'em in the hum of the planets,
in the songs of the stars
that carry the cadence of time.
Hear your grandaddy in the high fiddle string,
your rogue uncle in the banjo ring,

your button-shoe aunt in the corner guitar
keeping time   keeping time   keeping time.
Hear 'em in there 'cause that's where they is!

My people was music.
They didn't have no politics, nor economics.
They didn't write no newspapers, nor history books.
That's not how their legacy is kept.
Their lives are the poems of my soul,
and the songs of my breath.

My people was music,
and if you wanna know,
you got to be able to *hear…*

The Comin' Home

I thinks one reason
I be leavin' alla time
is 'cause
the comin' home
feel
so
good.

Heir

The old man
comes in his sleep to
interrupt me,
to remind me of my sleep.

He holds me with sated eyes.
His face tells me
compels me
to breathe the mountain.
To feel the sting of stream
and slap of free winter wind.
To recognize sign of passing time
as easily as deer trail
or bear track
or turkey scratch.

His hands
remind me I have touched,
sketching with the strings
of banjo and fiddle
the flight of eagle and osprey
and splash of hickory trout,
unlined and easy
against a worn canvas.

His voice
leads me to hear
all things holy and unholy
in places only gods could worship
or lose their faith,
and men just stand
and live.

To turn from him,
seek young men
with clear eyes

smooth faces
strong voices
and a firm grip on new directions,

but always the old man,
the old man comes,
and I cannot neglect,
cannot ignore.

In the Cabin

Out here
the moisture in the air freezes
right in front of your eyes.
It sparkles all around you in
the astonishing light
of the full chrome moon
and lifts you
up
and
up
into the unimaginable stars.

From here you see
through those frozen ivory sparks
the blacksnake road,
the sword-glint of Big Laurel
twisting under dark patches of pine,
an owl
slicing over shimmering fields
fading into the silent heart of night.

From here
somehow
you see.

In the cabin
the fire burnin'
Dave fiddlin'
the bottle hangin' between hands,
Now just a spoonful boys...
The worn wood curve of the cane
dark-stained from the oil
of the old man's hand.

Sherman laughing,
his crackling eyes
choreographing
fire-dancing, diamond notes
shot from Tim's vibrant banjo,
Mike's breathless mandolin.
Crystalline-iced windows
by stuttering lamps
mirroring the scene
back onto itself
in sheets of silver
and shafts of flickering light.

This will stay.

From here
somehow
you see,
this,
all this,
will stay.

You turn,
open the door.
In the cabin
Dave fiddles,
the fire
burns.

Sherman Hammons — 1903-1988
A Toast

Here's to the rivers
The runs and the streams
That flow from the heart
Of a mountaineer's dreams.

Here's to the fish
The birds and the game,
And a pioneer spirit
That never was tamed.

Here's to the fiddle
And banjo that rang,
And the tunes that he played,
And the songs that he sang,

And the stories he told
Under clear open skies
With the moon in his voice
And the stars in his eyes.

Here's to a life
And a time that won't end.
Here's to Sherman,

And Amen.

They's Music Tonight

Feet slap time on the old slab floor,
Moon glow slips through the puncheon door,
Fiddle bows dance in the orange firelight—
C'mon boys, they's music tonight!

Thumbs double-down on the high fifth string,
Fingers frail and the banjos ring,
Quart jars pass from hand to hand—
C'mon boys, it's a hot-time band!

Mouth set up in a crooked grin
As the notes fly out of the mandolin,
Ears wide open and eyes shut tight—
C'mon boys, they's music tonight!

Wrist bent hard 'round the guitar neck,
Pick blurs quick in a fancy lick,
Sound box sends out a holy shout—
C'mon boys, they're a'bustin out!

Marthy Campbell and *Cumberland Gap,*
Swingin' On a Gate and *Fox Tail Trap,*
Old Plank Road and *The Girl I Left Behind,*
Get Home Cindy and *Evangeline*

Shoulders sway to the bass thump's boom
As the dancers whirl around the room,
Toes tap rhythm in pure delight—
C'mon boys, they's music tonight!

Hill Sailor

He was like the wood of the mast
he brought from the ship
to make the four foundation logs.
He saved the unsalted top
to spoke-shave the Norway Spruce
down for his fiddle-box.

The drone of the pipe was in his blood,
and he thought he'd left
his sea-legged jigs on the shore,
but as he sailed through the forest
with the thrush and the warbler,
he knew the mountain
remembered the dance of the sea,
and his songs flew
on the bowsprit of the Alleghenies.

The night the cabin was finished
a skeleton stood in the doorway,
didn't speak, cocked its bow arm
and played *Turkey in the Straw.*
When he woke, he wiped the sweat,
took down the fiddle,
tried it,
and never played it another way.

He laughed at the bubbling limestone spring,
the splash of summer,
the quickened color in the sap-drained leaf,
and cozied in the covering snow.
He seeded his joy into the land
and took it back at his pleasure.

They pulled the planks from his sea chest
to make his coffin,
played his tunes for a night and a day
before they laid the fiddle in with him,
and after they put him in the ground,
they marked the spot with a single straight cedar to the sky
pointed like a mast
on the mountain's horn.

The Fiddler

For Dave Bing

In his hands
they become alive.
The bow slips over the chords
like a tear on a cheek
or dances on the strings
like a baby's laugh.

Notes,
Like extensions of his love,
Swell the receptive heart and soul.

The rest of us
think we know.
We dance, and sing,
and enjoy life as best we can,
but the fiddler,
the fiddler now,
he *fiddles!*

In the Hills We Sing

Here in the hills
In the haven of home
We hold in our hearts
The songs of our own

Rhythm of forest
Cadence of stream
Caught by the bow
The sound-box and string

Here in the hills
We have suffered and loved
Black rivers below us
Black mountains above

Coal in our veins
Timber our limbs
Out-pouring our glory
To our gods and our sins

Here in the hills
The life-songs of years
Stay long on our lips
Linger loud in our ears

With voices sent straight
From the soul of the thing
Here in the hills
We sing!

February on Williams

Under the ice
the river slows,
above, mist rises
snow falls.

The shining, sluggish prey
hangs in the congealing stream
reflected in the wise trout's eye.
Not yet.
Not yet.

Hard black mountain
stark white sky.
Wind whips shades of gray to blue.
No animal moves.
The birds are still.
The gods
lie silent, and buried.
Not yet.
Not yet.

Under the ice
the river slows,
above mist rises
snow falls.

Cold Run
For Mike Bing

Here
I have always been.

Here
is my soul
in the stone.

Here
is my heart
in these beeches
spared the saw.

Here
is my soft flesh
sunken into this hemlock
so long fallen
the rock has formed around it.

Here
is my vision
in this play of light through ice
draped on these white cliffs of bone.

Here
is my sound
in this music of water
plunging deep
over fall
after fall
after fall.

If you ever have need of me
you will find me

here.

Crayon at the Sinks
(Porte Crayon at the Sinks of Gandy)

To get it right,
that scrub Red Spruce
has to move over
to the right side,
and the laurel has to
go to the left
and open up quite a bit,
let in more light
where the water goes in,
and under,
and disappears.

The height can stay the same,
the proportion is perfect
(you can tell God did that)
but this drawing is mine
and I can tell the story
any way I want
with my pencil,
parchment,
paper,
pen.

Let the damned photographers document—
        This is art!

the gendarme
(at seneca rocks)

high sky, soft wind
blue, blue, blue
in a mild summer

but the crack opened anyway
a small trickle of limestone,
pebbles at first,
not enough even to
make a noise

but then quick, quick
so fast a blink would miss it,
it fell,
200 tons of quartzite crashed
into the hemlock below

and before the sound
hit the valley
the debris had settled
and where it had stood
there was nothing,
no protection anymore,
no silent watching
to keep us safe
and we are left
uneasy, and fearful
unknowing
what will come next
or when.

Tao-Billy

Don't give me none of that
Tao-Billy/Hill-Zen stuff.

I just wanna reach down in my belly
and join in,
not just listen to,
the eternal laugh.

On Cranberry

The heartbeat of the wilderness
thrown from these electric fields
throbs through me
like the surging spring river.

Wrapped in the mountain's energy
I become receptive,
reading vital signals
from the vast obscurity
of the universe.

Thunder growls downriver
rolling like a ghost wagon
up the sides of the steep valley
galloping to a tremendous explosion over me
an incredible release around me
and I am scattered.

The flood flows from me
to the farthest echoes of the echoes
rising on the wind
spreading on the very soul of existence.

God, I'm alive!

I'm shining
in the everywhere
the always
of this world.

Scenic Highways

Concrete is manmade rock.

We harden the earth
and tie the hills
with ribbons of rock
fusing our futures
excluding no one except...

God is lonely
under bridges and over tunnels.
Few meet him there to see
the power in the mountain
the glory in the sky
or the kingdom
in a drop of rain.

I breathe infinity on the wind
and feel my reflection in this morning.

The Ground of Eden
Dual voice poem with Sherrell Wigal
Sherrell's poem on left, Kirk's on right

Go up the mountain
Go to the end of the road
Go to gray boulders of yesterday
Here, on the lip of the world Hesitate
Pause while the earth breathes around you
Inhales you
Exhales with you.

Starlight of millennia
Traveled here from ever
Angled through the hidden eyes of animals
Filtered through the ageless stone

It is dusk
And the dreams of almost-lovers
Hang like the shadows of children
Around the edges of night
A rabbit crouches
Unseen against a thicket of laurel
Her nervousness vibrates the mountain
Vibrates the humans who linger here

Found me here in this shadowed night
Thrummed into me the quasar pulse

There is a stirring
Maybe the boulders move
Maybe the spruce grows another seven inches
Maybe the world slips out of its orbit

The resonant wave
Of some authenticity
Started long ago

Listen
Listen for the whisper of night-wings
The ferns curling back upon themselves
This mountain moving with the galaxy

Some clear truth
I didn't know
I had always known

And if there is a touching
The forest will explode

Broke inside me
With a flood of certainty
Charged me with prismatic fire

Light of creation
Light of the scriptures
Light of a thousand promises kept

And everything changed
Light into mountain
Mountain into me
And I became...

This
This is the land which owns you
This is the ground of Eden
This is the soil
You cannot leave.

"Beware! Meat Eating Plants Surround You!"
(From a sign at the Cranberry Glades Boardwalk)

"The Pitcher Plant drowns and digests
its prey in rain-filled leaves.
The Sundew traps bugs
on its leaves' sticky hairs.

In this way, these plants receive
nitrogen and other nutrients
scarce in the bog's soil."

I sit beneath this sign
in Round Glade,
try to write

but I'm lost here again
drowned and digested
on this high limb of Kennison

my substance left here on the mountain
my nutrients let go

while my words
crawl off the page
into the Sundew's sticky hairs
trapped.

For Louise McNeil

I call no Muse…

they call me
speak to me in languages i don't understand
their history, poetry, dance, song
seep into me
hematite into rock
cementing me
like these mountains
long ago under the sea

For the sandaled foot should never tread
Where the brogan lumbers…

these ancient entities are older
than those nine Greek daughters
older even than their parents
sitting on Olympus
old gods throwing down form
and structure
rules to abide by
these ancestors know no rules
know there are no rules
to write it down
chain it
keep it from being

I have gulled the pith from a sumac limb…

the spirit of this place is wild
grows wild
sprouts up from the ancient seabed
now thrust high
grows up and out and away
from all that carbon sediment
shouts into this green world

becomes available and apparent
not withholding, not urging
just there
just there
waiting

To play a tune that my blood remembers…

my blood
"blood of my fathers"
blood in the soil
blood in the sky
rubbed into my hands
washed into my veins
running deep through
the hollows of my body
"back to the seed"
remembered in
the wind of my mouth
hawk cry
over big spruce
fossil on the broken mountain top
water crashing in pools
below the middle falls
moving toward and away from
always toward and away from
my self.

Watchin' the Sun Come Up on the Highway

The night
just kinda backs off and says,
"You think you've seen something?
Well, watch this!"

Just before Ol Sol starts up
over Big Spruce
you always say,
"Hell, it's mornin' in Buckeye."

And someone says,
"Oh, that's real good, Judd.
It was morning 45 minutes ago in D.C.
and about 5 hours ago in Liverpool."

He slips on over the mountain
and just fills you up.
This is ever bit for you, babe!
One more day.
All you see is yours.

Anybody who can sit
and watch the sun come up
and not say thank you
has no idea
where he's come from
or where he's going.

May 7th, 1990
On the River

Last night,
it snowed.
Mice got into my groceries
and I got drunk and locked my keys in the truck.

This morning,
it was cold
and I felt bad
I had to wade snow
and bust a window outa my truck
before I could go anywhere.
Being stupid is gonna cost me
and I can't afford much.

But,
this afternoon,
I saw an osprey
and wood ducks and a red fox
and three bear and a bald eagle!
And before dark
I caught a trout
big enough to make my supper.

This evening,
as I walked back to camp,
the moon threw my shadow
and flashed through the ice on the trees
and put on a show
Broadway will never know.

It was a good day.
I put out the leftovers
for the mice.

senior took exception
(a found poem)

on the old main road north
outa the town of lost creek, wv
there was a sign,
a big new lighted electric sign,
about 4 foot high and 6 foot long,
on which you can arrange black plastic letters
to spell out anything you want to say.

for two weeks, i drove by that sign
and it read, on both sides,
"Tommy Jenkins
  is a liar, a cheat,
  and a thief"

then one day, i drove by and it had changed!
then it read, on both sides,
"Tommy Jenkins *Jr.*
  is a liar, a cheat, and a thief"

Rural Romance
(a found poem in February)

!! MOUNTAINEER GUN SALES !!
Ammunition!
Live Bait!
Valentine's Day Gifts!

911 Call Log
Fairmont Times-West
Virginian September 28, 2012
(a found poem)

8:30 PM -
Shots Fired -
Serene Street -
Pleasant Valley

Item: Art and Madness Linked
(a found poem)

Well, noooooooooooooooooooooooooooooooo shit

Visitin' Charleston
(for a poetry reading)

What you do is
if you're comin' West on 60
and you run outta gas on top of Gauley Mountain
you just don't hit your brakes
and if you catch all the lights right
well where you stop rollin'
why that's Charleston.

When you get there, stay low.
Don't show 'em too much,
just get your timing down,
tell 'em what they wanna hear.

What you'd really like to do is hit the streets.
Slip outta that poetic mellow
and kick into a primordial chain-saw screamer.
Just rip the bars all night
and then bounce into the bus station for breakfast
in the morning with steam comin' off your shoulders
and nobody wantin' to get within ten feet.
Feel that satisfying glaze of fear
comin' over what's left of your eyes
while the gravy dries in your mustache.

When they ask you why,
just tell 'em what you said before;
"It's more fun than bein' *happy*."

Emotional Security at a Reading

I wonder

if I'm the only person here

wondering

if I'm the only person here

wondering

if I'm the only person here

wondering?

Robert Bly's Question
at my reading

"How did you learn to do that?"
he asked.

"I didn't,"
I replied.

witness at the kitchen window

a murder of crows in the backyard.
a lone rabbit in the fog seems suspect.
the hummingbirds ain't talkin'.
the sun courts morning,
arresting the day—
light breaks and enters,
laying down the law.
shadows in the doorway
commute the sentence.
this summons serves us all.

May 1, 1984

No clouds.
Good sun,
but the sky still high enough
to chill as the sweat dried.

I turned off the mower
drank from the hose
and everything was so damned sweet
I just wanted to lie down
under the lilac
and drown
in the heavy air.

I did.

that rene` descartes, what an elitist, ya know?

i think, therefore i think.

i am, whether i think or not.

i think.

If You Can See the Edge, You're Not on It

Here,
tightroping along the abyss,
where balance is all,
you only begin to gain balance
when you begin to quit
expecting to fall.

It is not always a wise man
or a strong man,
but it is necessarily a brave man
who shakes hands with God
and then lets go.

My angels are of the earth
golden men who rose from the clay
lost their hair
and began to think.
I speak to the ones near me when I can,
remembering that knowledge is new as well as old,
remembering I am of them,
remembering where we are from

I will be the angels
to the ones who come after me
when they remember what they are of
and where they are from.

Here,
between,
is the dangerous path
that offers no resistance.
Here,
I will cease the struggle
to gain the balance,
walk the edge,
and whatever is to be done,
I will do.

Planting

There is one who lives alone.
His love comes down like lightning
from the depths of his sky
into all he sees.
It spreads and spends its power
in strokes on the canvas
and does not return
leaving him
always
empty
and afraid.

My father
shuffles across the hospital floor
on bruised feet
and swollen legs.
His full-choke arteries
unload 12-gauge chunks of cholesterol
into his brain.
Here and there.
Little by little.

In his eyes
I see the athlete's pride,
the graceful strength
and fluid stride.
In his eyes.
Under his pain.
"How can you stand it?" I want to scream.
"How can you stand it in there?"
I cry in the elevator.
I never saw him run.

My daughter
stares at me
with her sister's eyes
her mother's eyes
my father's eyes
and I don't know
whose child is whose.

By them all I am fixed to the canvas.
By them all I plant, and am planted.

When these parts of me are taken away,
when these parts of me are gone,
what will be left to shadow the light?
My love has not returned.

From beyond my fathers
to my daughters
and beyond,
in the sweeping, twisting frame,
all there will be
under the air
almost unheard,
the slow rolling thunder,
the slight echo
of my seed.

equinoctial

redbud winds through blooded limbs
willow light over butter fields;

hawk cry	sparrow song
river rush	mud smell;

veins swell	senses grow
yellow leaps	purple spurts;

color steeps the air with the juice of life.

earth absorbs us,
fills our mouth and eye
laughs in our ear
sings in our skin
breathes in our mind,
and spins on into the green dream.

March

how the forsythia already knows,
and lets you know
it is going to be that color
even before it shows
its blooms under the snow.

the daffodils, too,
slightly paler,
but secure in the knowledge
of their particular yellow.

even the fruit trees,
the cherry and peach
are confident by now,
smug in that perfect pinkness.

but oh, that crocus…
you know it has to be
so much fun
not knowing your color
until you lift up
and see
the sun.

The Sound Snow Makes

This warm June afternoon,
in the too-hot sun,
by the too-noisy falls,
with bird-song rivering
around my ears
on the too-busy wind,

I remember—
the sound snow makes—
when the river is frozen
and the sun is cold
and the birds and the wind are gone,
everything as still as Death's eye—
when the frigid air cracks your vision
and the breath is solid in your lungs,
you can hear it
splitting the night,
spilling out of the sky
in torrents of white.

When you have learned to hear nothing else,
and you're just about to believe you can,
you can.

here you are

this morning
i watch the water chase and swirl
in the river's necessary descent.

the sun is up, and
something immediate and important
is happening here—

winter's ghost leaving the trees,
spring conjuring itself
in purple swellings and whispers of green.

i toss a rock into the run
aware its landing is crucial
in every scheme of things—
new shelter for mussels that
become food for crawfish that
become
food for trout that become …

    i remember the walk
    up cold run when i stopped
    to look at a lily

    a different and further
    color than i ever had seen
    and back-stepped into the stream.

    i lifted my foot,
    watched the print fill,
    knew everything changed.

    my grandson was born
    because of that step, and
    so were you.

light bounces off
the water's play,
blinds the hawk,

saves the pine squirrel
running out the limb
to investigate the splash.

no brook trout now,
so i move upstream,
catch a nice brown.

because she's stock
i decide to keep her,
clean her for supper.

because of that,
i cross to dig ramps
and gather mushrooms.

more footprints fill,
the sun warms,
buds burst.

each of these things
immediate and important and irrevocable
in history will matter.

       you may not believe the story
       about cold run and the lily
       and you being born,

       but i really did that,
       i really did,
       and here you are.

seeing god on the interstate

two hours of driving
has warmed the air inside the car,
excited the apple's aroma
from the seat beside me.

high in preston county, west virginia
the sun breaks
from the storm clouds
and floods the hills
the cut farms
the swollen spring rivers
with that incomprehensibly beautiful
yellow light,
like september,
only now
now!
and i am stunned again,
as i am
each morning's drive
or evening's walk,
with how blessed,
how blessed
we are
with what we have been given.

Outside In

(for Wilma Acree)

outside
smooth shell
impenetrable
no windows or doors to
open
to reveal

inside
under amniotic film
an embryo waits,
pulsing yellow,
for the spark of life
that signals – begin

outside
skin holds together
blood and bone,
tissue and tendon.
fully formed
i walk among the living

inside
i pulse
keep the secret close
gather yellow sparks
behind closed windows
wait to be born.

Understanding Georgia O'Keefe a Little Better

On the road from Albuquerque
just south of Santa Fe
the sun set
and the light changed
into something breathing
I could hold in my hand,
could sift through my fingers like
orange, orange water
or sand.

And I saw.

"Five-Planet Dance Wowing Stargazers"

*"Saturn, Jupiter, Mars, Venus and Mercury are line-dancing, mingling,
and conjuncting, in a diagonal slash across the sky that earthlings have
not seen since 1940 and will not see again until 2040"*

The Washington Post, April 23, 2002

epigraph
(from the same article)
"There's nothing you can learn by looking at it."
Bob Bolster, Hopewell Observatory

sub-title
the difference between art and science

everything i know,

i learned
by looking at it.

Are You Listening?
Palm Sunday/Passover/The Full Crow Moon 1994
(for Boyd Carr)

Okay okay.
My shingle is out
and the gloves are coming off.

There are people out there
who still embrace concrete.
They think that by surrounding themselves
with things they believe have permanence
they somehow solidify their own.
What a waste of energy.
Even though
our galaxy and thousands of others
are moving at 360 miles per second
toward something out there
that itself is moving toward
or away from
something else.
Even though
we always obviously have known
time is just something somebody made up.
Einstein just had to convince the schoolteachers.
Maybe that took genius.

I have pulled my ladder up.
I am out of the earth.
My sound is from the water
given to you
through the air
soaring towards the fire.
I am not diminished by any of those elements,
and they are not diminished in me.

The truth has nothing to do with this
and that's the truth.

The mythology is what's important.
These poems will be written.
These pictures will be drawn.

I have heard the stone.
I have felt
in the winter chill
the river freezing from the bottom up,
my own stream hardening in me
but still flowing,
still flowing.
I have seen whirls of stars
forming in your breath,
angels dropping
from the pockets of your overalls.
Around you,
I have tasted the birth
of the lambent flame.

Now listen, here's the thing—
All rocks
are now the art in the road.
The patterns I see are yours
as surely as they are mine.
Every stick
is carved by the blade without knowing,
holding all the knowledge close,
unspoken in the myth.
The mythology is what's important.
The idea of
the mythology is what's important.

My shingle is out now
because I'm afraid I understand
and you
had everything to do with that.

Voyager
Petroglyphs at Salt Rock

With all the technology and skill they could muster,
they left here, on the rock,
birds, and turtles, and deer,
and a map of the river valley,
and a picture of me.
They sent it hurtling through time to proclaim

> "This is who we are
> and where we live
> and what we have."

Skipping past the last planet's influence,
the spinning craft flashed into the free universe.
It contains recordings of our music and our mathematics,
expressions of our poetry and science,
a map of our solar system
and a picture of me.

Built and launched
with all the technology and skill we could muster,
it screams to the scintillant stars,

> "This is who we are
> and where we live
> and what we have."

"I am here." this poem says.
I sent it to tell you of this time,
of this arrogant yet beautiful species of being.
We are capable of great grace, and great terror,
in touch with timeless wonder
but holding this planet hostage to our social whims
while we slowly realize our relationship with the whole,
our brotherhood with each other
with every shining part, from the bird on the rock

to the laser dance of the spaceship,
each thing born of the blinding bright crack of the void
each thing carried in the common heart of each one,
each thing reminding us,

> "This is who we are
> and where we live
> and what we have."

It is not hard to see myself someday
trying to translate this,
contemplating the me who wrote it,
wondering in subdued awe,

> "What was he thinking,
> where did he come from,
> and where did he go?"

Spring Prayer on Bald Knob

I pay $4.50 to ride the chairlift to almost the top
because I'm wiser now.
Some might say, "Nah... older."
I might say the same thing,
but I know which.

I walk directly to the trail head.
I've never been here
But I did look at the map this morning.
Two steps in and already I see a fossil
In the broken sandstone,
Calamites reminding me.

The first 3/8 of a mile drops off the ski trail
Through high hard woods.
Not much out yet up here,
Some violets and bluets, coltsfoot of course, and sarvis.
A few anemones trembling in the wind.
Trout lily is up but not in flower.
I lay my hand on an old cherry,
An older oak, an older still beech,
Thanking them for welcoming me in.
I'm not an old hippie or a tree-hugger,
I just know where I am.

I make the sharp left, hit the gas line,
cross the top of the hollow in sunshine and start the climb.
It feels good to be walking in boots again.

In the open, there's more out
The high bush blueberry is everywhere, just starting to bloom
And there's red and pink underneath I can't place.
I'm not smart enough to know 'em all,
But I'm smart enough to bring the field guide.
Wild bleeding hearts! Don't guess I've ever seen them.
And fringed polygala - small, fragile wings
gliding low over the mountain.

What a great planet...

It starts to get steep,
and I'm climbing hard now,
moving up, climbing hard
and moving up toward the bald
when the ghosts appear.
Richard gone 11 years now
And Mark exactly one.

They many times come like this,
When the experience is intense,
And memory hard against me.
The mirror haunting the frame,
It is never not there,
But I'm glad to have it . Always.

The top.
Scrub Red Spruce, rocks and wind—that's all.
Big wind. And a spectacular view
Of the whole oval of Canaan Valley.
I take off my pack and my hat and
move over to the edge.
I can almost lean out and let the wind hold me.
Almost.
I spin and take in the 360°,
shouting poems at the sky
when I realize the wind (or Richard and Mark)
has taken my hat halfway back down the trail.
I laugh and stumble after it,
Breathlessly complimenting them on the joke.

I make it back to the peak
And now begin to understand how awed I am.
I start the prayer.
I have no tobacco, so I offer water
The only valuable I have with me.
I gave my self years ago.

I turn to the four directions,
spill from the bottle
over my hands
onto the ancient rock.
It cleanses.
For a long time I breathe with the mountain.
For a long time the mountain breathes with me.

The way down
Circles under the crest
And slides along past another ski trail.
An easy walk
Through high pasture.
I pass an old orchard,
And spot two small apple trees in bloom.
Good. There will be food.
It will take a while, but that's ok,
I'm nourished now.

Those were prayers of thanks
Back there on the top.
I threw them out
To old mother earth and old father sky
And do you know what they did?

A full plush cover of spring beauties
carpeting the meadow path
edge to edge
All the way down.

Birds Gathered Early

This year,
Summer just started it seems,
the birds are gathering early,
here still in July,
not really starting to move,
just flying now together,
just beginning to hear the air
that tells them it is time to prepare,
to get ready to go.

Wet this year,
storms and floods,
rain and rain and rain.
Perhaps that pulled the trigger,
braced the climate,
charged the atmosphere with the call,
told them in soft cicada voices,
"Now."
"Now."

I see them.
I know them.
I know their instinct,
know the pull and draw,
know the way without knowing;
know the price of leaving,
know the cost of coming home,
know this year
I will go with them.

Waiting to Hear You Say
What I Already Know

I remember the smell of rain
pushing east up the mountain,
following the birds
moving ahead of the front,
pulling thunder from
the cumulus sky,
sending me scurrying
down the lee side,
seeking shelter,
saving myself,
wanting just the hint
of the storm
to be the only thing
to fall over me.

I walk

to the edge of the world
and back,
each day new,
new passage through this old realm,
everything known refreshed,
sensed now with reclaimed vision the
elegance of lilies—
recalled in my touch and taste and smell
the mercy of earth, the uplifted air—
the pure grace of rain
heard again in these quiet ears.

Bridges

tie there to here,
was to is
over spaces we cannot reach by ourselves.

now, because we know,
we stop on each one to kiss
and steal time from underneath
to line our pockets

our watches have stopped
so we simply move down the path
letting the new flow up from the banks,
shift in our direction and push us on
to the next,
and the next

a river of color

there is one red apple in the tree.
it is the shade of the feeder on the porch,
the sweatshirt you're wearing.
hummingbirds helicopter out of the forsythia,
rise and hover in front of the fruit,
sway and dart,
dip and chase,
move to the feeder,
to you on the swing.

gnats float on the moist current,
move up and down
in rhythm with our blood,
the pulse in our fingers
passes through the skin
as the gnats pass each other,
bobbing in the blue morning
over the verdant fencerow
where last night the air hung white
above the dodder's pale lace,
waiting for the sky to lose the light
and darken to the color of earth and us.

after dark,
glowworms glittered green,
winked thin laugh lines
under the peavine and ivy,
under the porch steps,
under our eyes.

now, fragrance from some yellow-leafed limb
vibrates a crack in time,
hums memory in my glistening vision,
recalls the smell of split wood,
orange oak flesh from a past visit
when i needed warmth

and took the tree's gift twice,
once in the cutting,
again in the stove.

you push poems from the page,
lush lines temper our senses
the way the wood healed the silver chill.
we cast word spells on each other throw
them around this singing space,
you by reading, me by listening,
both by knowing the poetry
of this moment in our breath,
in the scent of our skin,
in the spark of our eyes.

everything shudders.

the swing pulls the earth
around the sun.
the porch frames the circle
of the wheeling sky.
the fence holds the seed
of every wet, green
growing thing.
the rain shines substance
into the timid wind.
the tree offers the apple
to the sparkling day.

i look at you.
birds laugh their songs, and
god is a river of color in the
shimmering air.

Divide
(in the year of turning 60)

The current is strong against me—
Stronger the farther I go,
But the river bed is gravel,
I have good footing
And despite age and disease
My legs still have power;
I move forward.

The dry season has come
And the dugout canoe
Hung up in the shoals.

I got out to push,
To get past this hard place.
I have no idea how I'm going to
Get back in the boat.

      2 days ago, the canal guide said,
      "We are on the other side!"
      As the tour boat slipped
      Through the Gaillard Pass
      Across the Continental Divide.

      The mountain chain runs
      From Patagonia to Alaska
      Slicing East from West
      Through three continents
      South, North and Central America,
      And I have crossed over
      In a boat.

      It was easy.

      How did I do this?

I don't understand
How I got here.
I take a long look
Down both sides of the Culebra Cut

Where the waters of
Gamboa Lake mix,
Pour north
To the Caribbean,
South back under the Centennial Bridge,
The Pan-American Bridge
To the great blue Pacific.

Impossible,
But I have crossed over.

I know where I've been.
I see where I'm going.
It is a beautiful trip.

Of the nine in the canoe,
Five of us had to get out,
Including the Embera guide.

Now, of those, I'm the only one
Left in the water.
Old, fat white guy
In above my waist.
The Embera laugh,
A genuine laugh
(there is humor here)
And they are sharing with me.

I haul myself up
And in,
Swing my ass over the side
And slip back into the seat
Like I know what I'm doing.

Young Francisco smiles,
The only one in Embera Puru
With any English
And says,
"You made it."

I smile back.

November 14, 1970

The DC9 screamed into the hill
140 feet below the runway
and exploded
scattering naphthalene and classmates
over a good part of Wayne County.

All through the rainy night,
under the hum of high-tension wires,
searchers slogged through the crash site,
praying that they wouldn't find
what sickened them
when they did.

Dawn, and the weather broke.
The pylons of the power lines,
burnished like gun barrels in the sun,
glinted savagely into our eyes,
but that was not
what made us cry…

The Death of Her Son

She asked all her questions
in the unanswering hours,
after the preacher had gone
and the boys who brought the flowers
from the funeral home
and all the family and friends
who brought cakes and coffee
and all the food
in dishes with name tags
on the things that needed to be returned.

After she was alone,
unweeping and defiant,
she anticipated replies.

She talked to him
for weeks after.
He was with her.
She nursed him as a baby,
cuddled him as a child,
scolded him as a boy,
and argued with him as a young man.
Over and over.
Until
one day at dinner
she turned to speak to him

and saw his chair at his place
set with his plate and his knife and his fork
and she saw that he was gone.

The sorrow overwhelmed her.
She fell down and wept.
She felt him rise to leave
and, through her tears,
she saw him,
loved him,
and finally
let him go.

At My Father's Funeral

Before they took the body out
at the last family visitation
my aunt leaned forward,
motioned toward the front,
and whispered over my wife's shoulder,
"You know, his mother
was the one who insisted
on calling your husband 'Kirk.'
She died right after he was born."

My mother
turned and said,
"I think she just waited before she died
to make sure we didn't name him
after someone in our family."

When I looked
I saw her sitting on the wall
hovering just above the casket.
Our eyes met
and I heard her say,
just as clear as a bell,
"Don't you forget that."

I said,
when I caught my breath,
"I won't."

The Gift
(for Donnie)

To give to you
I would have to take from you,
reach down into your breast
and pull out the offending disease,
lay my hands on you
and draw through the gods of my fingers
the poison from the cells
like extracting venom from a snake-bite,
exhaling the bitter toxin
harmlessly on the ground around you.
I would have to take from you
to give to you
the only boon worth giving now.

But that is not mine to give.
I can only tender knowledge
of a gift already offered and accepted.

I can tell you
your happiness is in your daughter's laughter
your wisdom in her already too-discerning eyes
your spirit in the voice of the farm and the forest
your light in the streams and the sweeping skies
your touch in your husband's character
your love in the quilt of memory
you have stitched in our time.

I can tell you
your presence is deathless
in the hearts of those who know
the gift already offered and accepted.

The gift of you.

For Richard
(for Richard Black)

It's not much,
but the air is changed
now that you're not breathing it.
The streams
fall down the mountain differently now
that you're not standing in them,
trying to hit a trout in the head
with your sinker.
The deer are a bit more wary, somehow
already knowing
that someone else
who really wants to kill one of them
has taken your place in the woods.

It's not much,
but the light is harder now,
sharp off the bar,
unlike that soft, evil twinkle in your gaze
above another raised
short shot of Crown.
The catch is gone,
that hung moment
just before the joke was sprung
when you would clear your throat
and roll your eyes.

The music all hesitates now in places
as if pausing for you to whisper,
"Now just listen to this one".

The nights are all a little shorter now.
The fires all go out a little sooner.
It's not much,
but it's everything
and it's forever,
and we miss you.

Joe

(Baber Mountain 1990)
For Joe Barrett

Drunken pirates of the highway
We fell laughing from the van
Locked arms
And danced in an opium dream
Until the red sun rose.
In the scream of the sky
We looked in each other's eyes
And understood.

Years later
We sat under the Bodhi tree in the rain
On a street corner in downtown Lexington,
Me in your hat, you in my coat,
Backed against the night-soaked bricks
Until the wine was gone.
You wouldn't let me leave
And I wouldn't let you stay.
Finally, I picked you up
To carry you away before the police arrived.
You said you wanted to fight me
Because I lived in all worlds.
I said I wanted to take you home
Because you lived in none.

We were friends in there where we were.
I felt every pinprick syllable you wrote.
Every sharpened phrase thrust into the wood of life
As if you were holding off
The same demons who dressed your edge.
You couldn't climb out of there.
If not by Joan,
Then certainly not by me,
Or by any of the love thrown around you
Like gauze on a flame,
Never touching the clear light of your fire.

All I have of you
Is all there will ever be now.
It is not enough.

On the mountain,
I laid my cheek on the cool grass,
Closed my eyes,
And in each unmeasured pause,
Listened for your voice
One last time.

Appalachian Senryu

No answer to my call.
On the floor, the drugs
and the overturned cup.

Stones on the Slope
(for Mark Blain)

Stones on the steep slope,
more leaning than standing,
more leaping than falling
down with the sunlight
dappling the red trillium blooms,
purple here, purple everywhere
down to the gorge's floor
and the stream
where I'll put your ashes.

The North Fork
runs away with you,
beech leaves humming John Prine tunes
lift the scent of aged moss
and the rum I drank from
before I poured the rest
into the bend I dropped you in,
the small falls that carried your descent.

I sat on the stones,
the cool, hard ground,
backed against the rough bark
of the hemlock,
watched until the last of you was lost,
and said, "Good-bye, Mark-O, goodbye"
as the mountain said,

    hello,

       hello,

          oh…

Poetry Class
(for Irene McKinney)

this morning
gray light, and rain.
i laugh at the clock,
smile at the pillow
and miss breakfast.

today
i wrap poems around me.
sherrell and ed and susanna and john
blanket me with words.

now
they soak into my skin,
fill me with wonder.
"be happy", irene says, dying.

Farmer
(after the death of his wife)

He stops
for a moment,
leans on the hoe,
wipes the July sweat,
and suddenly remembers
this year it will be his daughter
canning the tomatoes
or someone else.

He stops
for a moment only,
today the garden,
but tomorrow
will be dry
and there is
hay to cut.

A Small Glow
(for my mother)

Sometimes…
Sometimes
There is a small glow,
Just visible,
Just there
Around your granddaughter's smile,
The bunting on the fencepost,
Your wife's shoulder,
That apple in that basket,
The whole damned mountain in September.

You can see it…
      YOU can see it
Because your mother taught you
– Look.
Look at everything.
And then
      Look a little more.

Driving Into Green
(for Bob Snyder)

Leaving here,
here where I always come,
here where I came to let go of Joe
and Richard and all of the others,
here where I came to let go of you,
I see no blue.

I hear no blue.
No Stoneman fiddle slides
as he slumped down the wall of the 'billy-bar
trashed into that musicians' ghetto of soul.
No Slim and Slam jazzed,
redded into purple,
blues pushed down
into the Avocado Seed Soup Concerto
underground in the alleys and back lots
and never imagined to be real.
No Armstrong, Martin, or Bogan,
ripping through the blue-black coal fields
and red-light gin joints
with strings pulled from the guts of old time
raggers and jazzers and balladeers.

No blue.

Not up here in this thin air.
Not up here in this pale sky grayed
from edge to me to edge,
holding the hope of the world in that flat cloud file
saucered with the stuff of life,
waiting to tip and spill
back into the tune,
blending airs and airs and airs
dropping them down
note by note
like shattered piano riffs

or broken mandolin runs;
like the ruins of symphonies.

Waiting to tip and spill
over me,
over this dark crest,
down the sides of this mountain,
down the sides of every mountain
running in streams
in rivers
in drains and ditches
into the open obscure maw of earth
to coil and collect
in secret stations
just below the roots,
just before the feeding.

This is the poem.

They will write about you.
And this is what they will say.

"You are not gone,
but you are with us always.
We hear you and feel you all around us
and we know.
We thank you for then
and we thank you for now
and we love you more and stronger
every time we hear a poem,
every time we read a line."

And they will not know why.

This is what I know.
This is all I know
coming down off this mountain
for the first time without you.
Spiraling down from the thin gray and brown,

no blue,
winding down through the blossom and bloom
of this warm and early Spring;

I have spilled from the sky.
I have run down the mountain
into the secret earth.
I am coiled and collected,
ready to feed this season
and all others forever,
ready to pull myself through the sucking roots
and give myself to the light and the life;
to the vibrance
to the shimmer
to the color of the world.

I met you here and meet you still
in these places;
feel your energy and your essence
in the synapse of knowledge
between cloud and raindrop,
between damp earth and moist seed;
in the brilliant chemical flash
of recognition when I see your eyes,
hear your voice,
understand your wisdom,
in the stirring of a cell.

This is what I know.
This is all I know
spiraling down off this mountain,
winding down this empty sky,
humming down,
coming through this eternal Spring,
jazzing down,
bluesing down,
driving into green.

Nothing Loved Dies

Nothing loved dies.

A Child in a Strange House

And so
I am here again
a child in a strange house
unsure of my existence
in an unfamiliar place.

With my poor power
I created illusions,
carving my familiarity
into the parts of this place
that made it mine
but
the parts are rearranged.
I am still the child
and this is still the house
but it is changed now
and changing
and I am not unafraid.
This place is not mine
to make or unmake.
This is not my world.

Here and there
stray gods stumble in the street
absorbing the little light
shimmering their ancient knowledge in the alleys
sighing their secret names in the night.
I cannot call on them.
My gods have no names.

I will set my shoulders to the strangeness
and learn to live
a constant stranger.

There Are Men Who Live Their Entire Adult Lives
Under the Streets of New York City
Seven Stories Below the Lobby Level
of the Waldorf-Astoria

You wear your days
sharp as scalpels
against the fragile veins.

Scream at them from
street corners
that
clocks are liars
or
god is an aspirin

And they will not listen to
or cannot understand
the noise in your eyes
as they push you down
beneath the streets

and leave you there.

On Asking a West Virginian How She Injured Herself
Badly Enough to Require Surgery
While Celebrating Her 60th Birthday in Las Vegas

(a found poem and a direct quote)

"Well,
I guess I shoulda listened to 'em
when they told me
to watch out for them
Cirque Du Soleil men."

A Conversation (One-sided)
Between the Federal Government
And a West Virginian —
That Is, If Anyone Ever Asks

(with the understanding
that a higher percentage of West Virginians
have died in military service to this country
than any other state population)

Well, I guess we're gonna have to
talk about it sometime.

I just don't know what it is you want me to be.
What you want me to stand up to.
Or what you want me to lie down for.

I tell you what,
I'll vote for your presidents
and fight your wars
and play your other silly games if
you'll come and take back
those bombs you dropped
on Logan County in 1921.

You are exquisitely arrogant
really and truly believing
that we could ever forget that,
much less any of these other things.

I am not your youth
or your conscience
or your scapegoat.

I believe
we'll both be better off
if you just
leave me alone.

Family Reunion

Up from the Sandy Country to avoid indictment,
Probably one of the night-riders who stole horses
And sometimes sons
For the feared and hated Federal troops,
You should have moved.

Your son farmed some,
But mostly worked the new E.K. Line,
And dug coal from his little land
To feed it and his family.
A slide took his strength, and his legs.

His son didn't farm.
He worked the railroad too,
The E.K. and the C&O,
And finally the steel mill that grew by the river.
But he married a farm girl.
Her sweet German blood
Mixed with the rich, Greenup flood-plain soil
And she raised gardens, and grapes,
And a family.
And the bright fragrant poppies she loved
Grew where she said.
Their oldest daughter married a city boy, an athlete,
And late, had a son.

My father, the athlete, never spoke of his father
Another railroad man
Who, in a construction accident
Lost a leg and his responsibility
And died when the children were young.

Legends all told and retold
Around sweet corn and iced tea
And fresh beans and watermelon
Each of all my summers here in this place.
How it was. And how it still is.

The government steals sons.
And coal and railroad and steel
Reap the harvest of Ohio-shore gardens,
Pulling heart and power
From the patient, tired land.
Poor voices protest from the cut furrows
Opened to the feed the machine
With all the hollow sorrow of the
Crushed legs and broken dreams and blinded wills
Of every generation.
Voices only those of us with something left to lose
Can hear.

This is my home.
I cannot ask myself why I'm still here
When I close my eyes
And feel the blood in the soil
And the soil in the blood,
And see bright poppies
Glowing
In the descending sun.

The Campfires of the Hunters
(the economics of controlled harvesting)

At night,
The deer move out off the ridge to graze.
One of the older does raises her graying head to gaze
With silently accepting eyes
Far down the mountain at the blaze
Of the campfires of the hunters.
Tomorrow, they will kill her for food.

They'll need the meat.
The winter will be long and cold
And the high cost of fuel for heat
Will cut into the food budget.

The doe does not own the land on which she is killed.
The hunters do not own the land on which they kill her.
The State owns the land.

The State regulates the hunters
And they've purchased licenses to avoid fines.
When they've finished their hunt,
They'll return to their homes
And their jobs in the mines.
They mine the coal from under the land.

They do not own the coal they mine.
The Coal Company they work for
Does not own the coal they mine.
The Bank owns the coal.

The State sells the mineral rights of the land to the Bank.
The Bank leases the mining rights to the coal to the Coal Company.
The Coal Company mines the coal and sells it to the Power Company.
The Power Company burns the coal
And produces fuel to run the mines
And to heat the homes of the miners.
The Bank owns a controlling interest in the Power Company.

Now the fuel bills will be so high
Because the Power Company was granted a rate increase.
By the State,
Which sells the rights to the Bank
Which leases those rights to the Coal Company
Which sells the coal to the Power Company
Which is controlled by the Bank and regulated by the State.

The Power Company sells power
To the State, to the Bank, to the Coal Company,
And to the miners.

At morning, the miners
Come yawning from the shaft,
Dark, minstrel faces
With eyes that have seen
The hunters' fires.

Have They Now?

"The Mountains Have Come Closer"
                    —Jim Wayne Miller

Well no shit I reckon so!
They've done knocked 'em down enough
You can see over top of most of 'em. Have
you looked lately?
Hell, the backside of Gauley is *GONE!*

And that's not the worst. It's like that everwhere…
Flying over this country reminds me
Of the last line of that book of stories
By that schoolteacher over in Pocahontas County,
The one where the old fellers went
For a fishing trip into the back country
40 years after the last time they'd been.
It was all clear-cut.
When they topped Black Mountain
And looked over into that devastation,
The leader just said,
"Boys, I'm sorry I brung ya."
And they turned and went back the way they came.

I know what those ex-mountains look like.
Feel like.
I drove up on one down in Boone County,
Over near Big Ugly on the Lincoln County border.
I don't know what mountain it used to be,
But the bartender at Cadillac Jack's
Said it was the highest point in WV
Before they started working it. I liked that.
Everyone needs their own highest point in WV
Even if it ain't really.
Up there was one little Mountain Ash tree living
And everything else blasted all to hell.
When I tried to get out of the truck,

That mountain just **screamed** at me.
I got back in. It hurt. It hurt a lot. It still does.

I ain't gonna tell my grandkids about that.
Or about any of them mountain stories.

How I've stood in rivers
That froze from the bottom up.
Caught trout and a red fox with my bare hands.
Seen the Northern Lights wrap orange and green
Curtains all around me right where I was standing.
Watched the sun come up
On top of Big Spruce Knob
And saw angels streaming down in the yellow light.
Seen fire shoot from the bend
In the tail of that comet
From down in the Cranberry
When there was so much snow
Everything was white, white, white - even the river.
Talked to ghosts and God on Bald Knob.
Seen a waterfall frozen from the outside in—
Ice tower bluer
Than Sherman Hammons' eyes surrounding
The creek plunging 60 feet down inside.

Made love to a woman
With my back against the mountain
And felt the rock flow over and around us
As we both sank deep into the stone.
Watched notes come off a fiddle and rise in the air,
Lift me and the fiddler up with 'em,
Circle around us and fly off
Into the black, black sky,
Leaving us as breathless and giddy
As those eternal lovers.
And on a blue cold night on Red Lick
When the wind and snow blew so
That it held me up off the ground,
I called up the Devil outa that holler and he come

And I looked him straight in the eye.
And other things I don't know
How to talk about.

I ain't gonna tell my grandkids.
I ain't gonna tell nobody.
Shit, they wouldn't believe most of it anyway.

I'll be dead before they knock the rest of
These old mountains down.
I'm grateful for at least that.
But I know what is lost.

I don't want my grandkids to know.
I don't want 'em to grieve what they don't know.
What they never had a chance to know.

What them bastards have taken away.

CD Contents

Track 1
The High Country Remembers Her Heritage/
    Grumblin Ol Man and Growlin Ol Woman
Mike Bing—Mandolin, Tim Bing—Banjo, Danny Arthur—
Guitar

Track 2
Heir and In the Cabin/Jenny Lind and Liza Jane
Dave Bing—Fiddle

Track 3
Sherman Hammons 1903–1988/Muddy Roads
Tim Bing—Banjo

Track 4
They's Music Tonight
Tim Bing—Dancing

Track 5
Hill Sailor/Turkey in the Straw
Dave Bing—Fiddle

Track 6
The Fiddler/Dance All Night with a Bottle in Your Hand
Dave Bing—Fiddle

Track 7
Cold Run/Over the Waterfall
Mike Bing—Mandolin

Track 8
On Cranberry/Cranberry Rock
Tim Bing—Banjo

Track 9
Scenic Highways/Mist*
Bob Shank—Banjo

Track 10
The Ground of Eden Kirk Judd/Sherrell Wigal

Track 11
Watching the Sun Come Up on the Highway/Sandy Boys
Bob Shank—Banjo

Track 12
May 7th, 1990 on the River/Groundhog Stole A Broom*
Bob Shank—Banjo

Track 13
Visitin' Charleston/Last Chance
Mike Bing—Mandolin, Tim Bing—Banjo, Danny Arthur—Guitar

Track 14
Here You Are/The Sunflower Dance**
Bob Shank—Banjo

Track 15
Are You Listening/Shakin' Down the Acorns
Bob Shank—Hammered Dulcimer

Track 16
Voyager/SpaceTime*
Bob Shank—Hammered Dulcimer

Track 17
Spring Prayer on Bald Knob/Hymn For Ruthie*
Bob Shank—Banjo

Track 18
A River of Color/Aura Lee
Bob Shank—Guitar

Track 19
For Richard/Margaret's Waltz
Mike Bing—Mandolin

Track 20
Joe – Baber Mountain 1990/In the Meadow*
Bob Shank—Guitar

Track 21
Stones on the Slope/Mammaw+
Dave Bing—Banjo

Track 22
Driving Into Green/Drive++
Pops Walker—Guitar

Track 23
A Conversation…/Flannery's Dream
Danny Arthur—Guitar

Track 24
Family Reunion/Home Sweet Home
Danny Arthur—Guitar

Track 25
The Campfires of the Hunters/Campfire+
Dave Bing—Guitar

Track 26
Have They Now? Kirk Judd

Recorded at Otter Slide Studio
Engineered by Bob Shank Produced by Kirk Judd

All tunes Traditional except

*   Composed by Bob Shank
** Composed by Vess Ossman
+   Composed by Dave Bing,
++ Composed by Pops Walker

Scan the code to access the music files:

Download to your device

Extract the files from the zipped folder

Play the files in your favorite music app

NOTES

Heir and *In the Cabin*

These poems (and some others) are about Sherman Hammons, of the legendary Hammons Family of Pocahontas County, West Virginia. Recorded by the BBC and the Library of Congress, they were renowned for their music and storytelling. I was lucky enough to be friends with them, especially Sherman, for 17 years.

They's Music Tonight

I wrote this in my own workshop. It is a dance poem.

Hill Sailor

When this poem is performed with music, the name of the tune changes to whatever the musician is playing. I stole and combined several family stories in this poem.

Crayon at the Sinks

Porte Crayon was the pseudonym of David Hunter Strother, a 19th century magazine illustrator and writer, who captured many scenes in West Virginia, including the Sinks of Gandy in Osceola in Randolph County, where Gandy Creek flows underground.

the gendarme

For many years a rock formation known locally as "The Gendarme" stood at Seneca Rocks. According to Native American legend, as long as it stood, the land and people were safe. It fell.

The Ground of Eden

This dual voice poem originally was two poems, written by me and by my long-time writing and performing partner Sherrell Wigal. We found we had written poems about the same place in Pocahontas County at around the same time. Sherrell's poem, originally titled *Unseen Against a Thicket of Laurel*, appears on the left side of the page. My poem, originally titled *Little Spruce*, appears on the right side. It is a performance piece meant to be read in two voices.

For Louise McNeill
This quatrain prefaces McNeill's book *Gauley Mountain:*
I call no muse for the sandaled foot
Should never tread where the brogan lumbers
I have gulled the pith from a sumac limb
To play a tune that my blood remembers.

"blood of my fathers" is from her poem *Hill Daughter*
"back to the seed" is from her poem *The Long Traveler*

May 7th, 1990, on the River
These are all true stories.

All of the found poems are true stories and/or direct quotes. *Item: Art and Madness Linked* was the headline of an AP article written about a 10-year government-funded study at the University of Iowa's Writers Workshop.

Visitin' Charleston
This poem was written for and performed at my first reading in Charleston West Virginia in the early 1970's.

Robert Bly's Question
This is a direct quote question and answer from my conversation with Robert Bly after my reading of *The High Country Remembers Her Heritage* at the first Kestrel conference at Fairmont State University.

Voyager
Written after spending much time pondering some petroglyphs on the Guyandotte River in Salt Rock on the Cabell County/Lincoln County border. There are animals and objects, including what some say is a map of the river valley, and a 6-foot 6-inch figure of a man with braids crossing his chest and his palms facing forward in a universal sign of peace. Voyager was the name of the first dual

spacecraft that traveled outside of our solar system.Both contained discs with much information, including Da Vinci's well-known depiction of the human form.

A River of Color
Written on the porch of a fishing camp on the Greenbrier River in Buckeye, Pocahontas County. Dodder is a clinging vine of the morning glory family.

Divide
This poem was written after a trip to Panama that included a voyage through the canal, a trans-continental train ride, and a visit to a native village, Embera Puru.The Embera have lived in the jungle for hundreds of years. They have no written language. They are beautiful people.

Farmer
Written about my father-in-law, Bob Cunningham, West Virginia Farmer of the Year in 2011, as recognized by the West Virginia State Farm Bureau.

Have They Now
The great Kentucky poet Jim Wayne Miller titled one of his collections *The Hills Have Come Closer*. In that collection, he introduced his character, The Brier. The short story collection mentioned is *The Last Forest* written by G.D. McNeill, Louise's father.

ACKNOWLEDGMENTS

I would like to thank Cat Pleska, Keith Davis and all the folks at Mountain State Press for publishing the first edition of this collection and Hayley Mitchell Haugen and Sheila-Na-Gig Editions for publishing this reprint; extraordinary writer and human being Barbara Smith; artist, poet, and philosopher Boyd Carr; painter, photographer and musician Dave Lambert for the excellent photo- graphs; and Bob Shank, Pops Walker and all the musicians who helped with the CD.

I particularly would like to thank Sherrell Wigal, a wonderfully talented poet and person, for her willingness to proof, edit, and provide suggestions for this book; and for allowing me the honor of performing and creating with her over the past many years.

I can't express enough gratitude to Mike, Dave and Tim Bing and Danny Arthur for allowing me to hang around all these years just listening. I'm a lucky man.

the clean light
of
your fire

kj
on
joe B

Sheila-Na-Gig Editions

www.ingramcontent.com/pod-product-compliance
Lightning Source LLC
Chambersburg PA
CBHW060324130626
46553CB00003B/903